THE RIVER WHICH SLEEP
HAS TOLD ME

Ivano Fermini

THE RIVER WHICH SLEEP HAS TOLD ME

Translated from Italian by Ian Seed

Odd Volumes

of

The Fortnightly Review

CHAVAGNES-EN-PAILLERS

2022

ODD VOLUMES
The Fortnightly Review 96 rue du Calvaire
85250 Chavagnes-en-Paillers
France.

Odd Volumes are published for subscribers.
http://www.fortnightlyreview.co.uk/odd-volumes

ISBN 978-0-9997058-2-7

info@fortnightlyreview.co.uk

Translator's Notice:

I am grateful to the editors of the following publications where many of these poems first appeared: *the straw which comes apart* (Oystercatcher Press, 2010) (Peter Hughes), *Long Poem Magazine* (Linda Black and Claire Crowther), *Shearsman* (Tony Frazer) and *Poetry Wales* (Zoë Skoulding).

I would especially like to thank Michelangelo Coviello, Milo De Angelis, Lorenzo Enriques, Francesca Marotta and Emi Rabuffetti for all their encouragement and support.

I am heavily indebted to Milo De Angelis for his illuminating answers to my questions about Ivano Fermini, and to Emi Rabuffetti for talking to me on the phone from Milan at the height of the Coronavirus crisis there in May 2020.

— Ian Seed

Contents

TRANSLATOR'S
INTRODUCTION

I t was in 2010, when I was researching for my PhD in post-war Italian literature, that I first came across a handful of poems by Ivano Fermini in a little known anthology.[1] I was struck by their fractured, yet compelling and strangely beautiful language, and I wanted to read more. Fermini's voice is unique and immediately recognisable. It was only after some time spent tracking down Milo De Angelis, who was editor, mentor and friend to Fermini, that I discovered he had died in 2004.

Little is known about Ivano Fermini's life. As Milo De Angelis says (see my interview with Milo after this introduction), he was a 'man made of shadow'. However, the basic facts are as follows. He was born in 1948 in San Paolo, a small village near Bolzano in the Alpines. Most of his adult life he lived with his sister in a flat in a working-class area of San Siro in Milan. He suffered from recurring bouts of mental illness. Towards the end of the 1970s he joined the

---

1 *Italian Poetry 1950 to 1990*, translated and edited by Gayle Ridinger, co-edited by Gian Paolo Renello (Boston: Dante University Press, 1996).

'Niebo' group, which centred around Milo De Angelis, and included Emi Rabuffetti, Antonio Mungai, Alberto Schieppati, Giancarlo Pontiggia, Cesare Lievi, Marta Bertamini and Roberto Mussapi. The *Niebo* magazine, founded by De Angelis, ran to nine issues from 1977 to 1980, and published work inspired by visionary poets such as William Blake, Gérard de Neval, and Arthur Rimbaud.[2] Fermini himself was especially drawn to the work of Paul Celan.

Ivano Fermini's work was published in the fifth issue of *Niebo* in March 1978. He would go on to publish two collections, *Bianco allontanato* (Banished White, 1985), and *Nati incendio* (Fire Births, 1990). Both these collections are now long out of print. He remains relatively unknown, both inside and outside Italy. It is hoped that this collection will bring his work to both an Italian- and English-speaking audience.

From the early 1990s, Ivano Fermini withdrew from the world of poetry. He had previously published *La scorciatoia* (The Shortcut) in 1970, but disowned this as an error of youth. The poems in this English translation are all taken from *Bianco allontanato* and *Nati incendio*. I have taken the title *The River Which Sleep Has Told Me* from one of the poems in this collection, 'Great Fragment' (p. 79).

Written in a highly innovative style, Fermini's poems refuse any clear resolution or easy definition. In the words of Giampiero Marano, his poems are 'marked by a "circular

---

2 For more information about *Niebo*, see my interview with Milo De Angelis below, and a more detailed history at https://r.unitn.it/it/lett/circe/niebo.

violence" which undermines all the comfortable fixtures of the obvious'.[3] They work constantly towards a depersonalization of the poet in the sense of any kind of stable 'I', seeking to point towards an interior reality which is beyond the boundaries of normal language. In the words of Renello and Ridinger, Fermini's 'words might be compared to pieces of fall-out created by some Big Bang, which shoot off in every direction at varying speeds thanks to Femini's bending of the rules of Italian syntax to an extreme'.[4]

It is impossible in English to render the power of Ivano Femini's original in Italian. However, as Renello and Redinger also state, the 'juxtaposition of vivid images and "border line" mental states [...] comes through in English all the same'.[5] And even in translation, these poems, especially when read together as part of a kind of epic whole, yield their own rich combination of imagery and music to readers prepared to have their expectations disrupted line-by-line, word-by-word.

---

3 See http://rebstein.wordpress.com/2008/04/28/la-generazione-cancellata-ii-ivano-fermini/.
4 See *Italian Poetry 1950 to 1990*, p. 317.
5 *Ibid.*

AN INTERVIEW WITH
MILO DE ANGELIS

I *'d like to start by asking how you first came to know Ivano Fermini and his poetry?*

I met Ivano Fermini during the winter of 1977 in my home in Milan, at via Rosales 9. We were holding our *Niebo* magazine meeting, as we did every Monday – I'd founded *Niebo* a few months previously with a group of poet friends – when suddenly we saw Ivano Fermini arrive. He was reserved and kind, but determined, and he made it clear that this was the right place for him and that he'd be joining us for a while. Ivano was quiet and very attentive. His few interventions in our discussions were sharp and vivid, like his poetry. When we asked him if he wanted to read out something of his own, he said, 'I'm not ready yet, but next year I will be.' And indeed in May of 1978 – in the fifth issue of *Niebo* – his poems were published for the first time.

Could you tell us something more about Niebo, *the poets who were involved with it, and something about the atmosphere of the times?*

'Niebo' means 'sky' in Polish, and it's the name I chose for the magazine when I returned to Milan after a long stay in Warsaw. I chose this name in homage to the Polish symbolist poet Bolesław Leśmian, whose work I loved very much and to whom I dedicated the final issue of the magazine. But the title 'Niebo' was deliberately provocative in the face of Italian culture of the 1970s, which was entirely devoted to militant politics and the celebration of a 'civil' poetry tied to events. *Niebo* was animated by a romantic and unrestricted vision of writing, and by a metaphysical and existential tension unrecognised in that period, in fact a tension that we could define as 'celestial', not in a religious sense but as a perpetual and extreme interrogation of the meaning or non-meaning of human life. The *Niebo* authors interwove poetry with thinking, exactness of the poetic line with breadth of philosophical vision (Hölderlin, Lucrezio, Trakl, Barbu, Benn, Leśmian) based on the teaching of Friedrich Nietzsche, a thinker who was important to us. In this way the Italian poets proposed by us from time to time were a long way both from the avant-garde and from demonstrations of *engagement*. These poets explored the hidden places of life and the human soul, and their work grew from a sense of the tragic, which was always valued by the contributors to the magazine, including Ivano Fermini…

I was struck by your phrase that the poets who contributed to Niebo *'explored the hidden places of life and the human soul'. This is particularly true, I think, when it comes to the work of Ivano Fermini. His poetry touches something in the depths, where the normal usage of words is no longer adequate.*

It's true that Ivano Fermini's poems touch something in the depths, something which has never come to light and which Ivano explores with the spirit of a diver, determined to reach deserted, abandoned and terrifying places. Ivano is a specialist of the dangerous and he ventures into the most explosive areas of language and human experience. He seems irresistibly drawn – he, the poet of the 'uneven', the poet 'without hands' – by that which cannot be understood, by that which never achieves its goal, by that which remains incomplete and solitary. From this comes the *dramatic* tone of his lines, the sense of menace which is imposed on us, something terrible, which from one moment to the next could demolish the very basis of our existence.

Yes, Fermini indeed strikes me as a diver, and to reach the depths, he pushes the syntax of the Italian language to its limits and beyond, even in a deliberately ungrammatical way. That being said, there is also an oddly beautiful music in his poetry, and I find his fragmented images very compelling. There is even, I would say, a strong element of play in the way Fermini constructs his poems.

Fermini conducts a ruthless crafting of language. It is absolutely not 'experimental' work or a laboratorial exercise, but rather comes from a deep necessity to go down into the heart of poetic language in order to renew it from inside, even fracturing syntax and its normal uses – as you have observed – in order to dig out values which have been kept secret, and have remained, until now, unuttered. For Ivano, it's a question of naming things and each time finding the right word, which is to treat each single thing with its own *unique* name, that which entreats us and lies underneath dozens of other banal words, and which demands to be said with millimetric precision. And you're correct when you note that there is a smiling and even playful element there, and it's right that that's how it is. A pain which is entirely monotonous and the same as itself does not exist. Every 'dramatic' poet feels that his own drama is such within the deeper context of a joyful song.

Certainly, Ivano Fermini was not an 'experimental' poet in a post-modernist sense, which, as you say, is important to understand. For Fermini, the search for the right word and phrase (even if impossible because he was reaching for what cannot be expressed in language) becomes a mission which, I would say, is almost a religious one, and here we can compare him, I believe, to Paul Celan. Nevertheless, he is able to communicate – if we are patient with our reading of him and willing to enter his world (which is also our world underneath the superficiality of daily life) – a frame of mind in which everything is possible, including the most traumatic experiences. But his poetry is always beautiful.

Paul Celan was an author of fundamental importance to Ivano Fermini, who felt for Celan a kind of adoration and knew by heart many of his texts. For both of them, poetry was felt as a 'sacred' duty – as you have rightly observed – and both of them submitted their own language to an exhaustive work of subtraction, to an inexorable reduction to what was essential, to the nerves of the page. This use of the word, stripped down and devoid of any redundancy, can enter undiscovered areas of life and language. It penetrates them like a drill and overcomes the greatest barriers, the highest defences, opening a road for itself to new territories and unknown and surprising worlds. Here is that sense of freedom, exploration and discovery that we experience reading the poetry of Ivano Fermini.

I agree very much with what you say about the sense of freedom, exploration and discovery. Can you tell me which other poets were important to Ivano Fermini?

I would say, first of all, the Russian poet – loved and translated by Celan – Osip Mandelstam.

And then, in general, poets of darkness and the fragment, poets of vertical language and steep slopes: the Romanian Ion Barbu, the French poet Yves Bonnefoy, to whom two issues of *Niebo* were dedicated. And finally various authors working in German, from Friedrich Hölderlin to Georg Trakl, and from Gottfried Benn to Ingeborg Bachmann, who perhaps in part appealed to Ivano Fermini because he had some knowledge of the German language.

It's important to understand something of the poetic tradition out of which Ivano Fermini worked. As far as I know, he published only three collections in his lifetime: La scorciatoia *(The Shortcut), 1970, which I have never seen,* Bianco allontanato *(Banished White), 1985, and* Nati incendio *(Fire Births), 1990. I wonder why Ivano Fermini published so little in his lifetime and why his poetry is so little known.*

Indeed, Ivano Fermini published only these three collections, and he completely rejected the first one (*La scorciatoia*), keeping it hidden from everyone because he considered it to be an error of youth. Ivano gave the best of himself at the end of the 1970s and at the end of the 1980s, when he published his essential books, *Bianco allontanato* and *Nati incendio*. Even the writings found after his death – a series of fragments entitled *La luna spesso* (Often the moon) – are of modest value, a tired repetition of what he had already written. It's true that he published little. But personally I appreciate poets who are measured in the amount they publish, because they are austere with themselves and their poetry. As regards fame, one has to say that Ivano never looked for it. He was always a solitary person, a man made of shadows. However, it's also true that recently some young poets have rediscovered him, defining him as one of the most important authors of his time.

I'm happy that his work is being rediscovered. We know little about the life of Ivano Fermini. Can you tell us something about that?

Ivano never spoke about himself, never told us anything about his past, his affections, his loves. He had a kind of extreme reserve – even more so among men – that made him impenetrable. With Ivano we spoke about poetry and only poetry, even for hours at a time, pausing every now and again over an adjective. I know only that he lived with his sister in a working-class neighbourhood in San Siro, Milan, and every now and again – when it was his or my birthday – I went to his home to give or receive a gift. I know that he loved light athletics (I remember one of his poems was dedicated to the Ukrainian hammer thrower, Yuriy Sedykh) and that he'd taken part in athletics since he was a boy. One of the loveliest memories I have of our friendship was when we watched together the young Russian Volodymyr Yashchenko beat the world record for the high jump in Milan. But I also remember sadder moments, at the beginning of the 1980s, when I went to visit him at the Villa Turro psychiatric clinic, and found him swollen and stuffed with drugs. At the beginning of the 1990s I didn't see him anymore and knew that he'd cut every tie with the poetry world.

Thank you for this honest, vivid, and moving portrait of Ivano Fermini. By way of conclusion, I'd like to ask if you have any recommendations for those readers coming across his poetry for the first time.

It's been a pleasure and honour, Ian, to talk to you about Ivano Fermini's poetry and to make my small contribution to making his work better-known. To readers meeting his work for the first time, I advise you to abandon yourselves to the beauty of the images without looking for the usual logic of rational discourse, and to accept being borne away in a flight to the great kingdom of analogy, of which Ivano Fermini is a master: with a leap of language he suddenly joins things together which seemed far away from each other, but which, in the spell of the poem, find their subterranean closeness and discover that they are sisters, united by a deep current which has always existed in secret and which now comes to light thanks to the magic of poetic invention.

This interview with Milo De Angelis was conducted in Italian by email in May 2020.

Milo De Angelis lives in Milan, where he was born in 1951. He has published *Somiglianze* (1976), *Millimetri* (1983), *Terra del viso* (1985), *Distante un padre* (1989), *Biografia sommaria* (1999), *Tema dell'addio* (2005), *Quell'andarsene nel buio dei cortile* (2010), and *Incontri e agguati* (2015). His work has been collected in *Tutte le poesie* (Mondadori, 2017). His work is also available in English under the following titles: *Finite Intuition* (Sun and Moon Press, 1995), *Between the Blast Furnaces and Dizziness* (Chelsea Editions, 2003), and *Theme of Farewell and After-Poems* (University of Chicago Press, 2013).

FROM *Banished White*

istanti che mani senza . . . vigna ridere . . .
. . . . cristalli finissimi . . . .
per quanto io tingo la notte
sforbiciando il soffio e
urna dei nomi
uno zoccolo tiene
i corpi alti e scivolosi

instants what hands without vines . . . laughing . . .
. . . . finest crystals . . . .
however much I dye the night
scissoring the breath and
urn with names
a plinth holds
the bodies tall and slippery

sbrecciarsi nell'ampolla racconta queste dita
né mai alte all'amputazione del dizionario
fortuna e grazia e insieme le nuvole tramortirsi la lingua
un grido sulle tavole minori
mosche in cerca di una rosa
la morte che arriva alla luce scivolata azzerata

to breach the phial tells these fingers
nor ever long as the dictionary's amputation
luck and grace and together the clouds stun language
a cry on the smaller tables
flies in search of a rose
the death which arrives in the slipped zeroed light

come sia diversa
strada e stella come sia lieve
bottone ai becchi
nato
fate un parco….. chi getta una mano ai pesci…
e sono già dei pezzi piegati nelle scatole
in questa sfera piange
i capelli

how different
street and star how light
bud to lip
born
you create a garden….. who throws a hand to the
    fish…
and they're already folded pieces in tins
in this sphere weeps
hairs

strazi ormai pingui
mosse della matassa tra e
in cori di polso sereno
lei come scrive che scrive
la prima ciliegia fiondante

allora: in cartone di righe
sassi bianchi
salti
vorrà dire con gli occhi
se ancora socchiuso se
la fune che non manca la mano

now rich tortures
moves of the skein between and
in choruses of the serene wrist
as she writes so she writes
the first slung cherry

so: on lined card
white stones
leaps
which means with the eyes
if still half-closed if
the rope since the hand is not lacking

su una lunga sabbia
a rovescio
la carta che ultima spegne
i villaggi nel pugno

    vicino alla sutura

        degli indietro e dei sassi

        uno sbieco
        annuncia sempre
        come stavi con la stoffa a
            salire
        fossero cerchi d'aqua

ora la ruga che è la noce
è di notte con le dita
rallentando o sbucando

on a long sand stretch
upside down
the map which lastly switches off
the villages in your fist

    near the suture

        from behind and from stones

        a sideways look
        still tells you
        how you had the strength to climb
        if only they were circles of water

now the wrinkle which is the walnut
is of night with its fingers
slowing or emerging

immobili ami-schiuma

. . . .
anche l'ombra
si spoglia delle mele
e anch'io salutavo
  se qualcuno gridava
                  l'argento
                  è finito

motionless foam

....

the shadow too
strips itself of apples
and I too gave greetings
   if someone cried
                  the silver
                  has run out

si abbassa rapidamente sotto la vigna da torcere in cielo
ha un catino buio per le ciglia
ogni frattura delle colonnine apre
la bocca per formare l'incudine e soffiare
perché è mare e pomeriggio e grigio fanale
piccola tonda minestra che grida gli occhi

he ducks down fast under vines twisted in the sky
has a dark bowl at the edges
every slit in the half-sticks opens
his mouth in the shape of an anvil and to blow
because it's sea and afternoon and grey light
small round soup crying eyes

scrosci non diranno che ramo è venuto
ma nulla di grande freddo da morte accovacciata
questo è il rimbombo
e altri sono partiti su bianche bisce disgiunte
per terra un incontro è saliva di netto colore di collo

the thunder cracks won't tell which branch has fallen
but nothing with the great cold of death crouched
    down
this is the thunder's roar
and otherwise are the games with disjointed white
    grass snakes
on the ground a meeting is saliva with the clear colour
    of their necks

anche   se inquieto il cratere di limoni duri
le stanghe vogliono … minimamente dico laterale
l'arsura nelle briciole che lo sguardo non vede

e la mano non è lunga come la carezza grigia
degli spilli di essiccamento e ruota
sorso l'altra ghianda dei passi
s'intitola il marmo del forziere

even   if I disturb the large bowl of unripe lemons
the bars want... minimally I say to one side
the burning thirst in the leftovers which the look
    doesn't see

and the hand is not as long as its grey caress
of the pins of drying up and turns
a sip the other acorn of passages
entitled the locked marble box

il visigoto dal volto di glicine
le sole tenaglie che doveva
defilando dal fulmine
viene
tenuto nella neve
con mani di conchiglia e
parole che soffiano sull'alba
finchè radici teneramente si sollevano
inanellando
fuori

the Visigoth with a face of wisteria
the only pincers needed
unthreading the lightening
comes
preserved in the snow
with shell-like hands and
words which blow on daybreak
until the roots tenderly come loose
curl in rings
outside

arrivano le parole vestite di polvere a punta
quanto mai accesa l'mboccatura dei grani
è subito fatta una sabbia o mente impiccata
si aprono le fonti dei pungitori di valli eterno
mai dato in costole asciughi
e provenga di nuovo
che gli prenda la corda e la lasci martellata e indifesa
vinci sopra quegli occhi scoscesi
la struttura è di falco è d'argento

words arrive dressed in dust sharpened
however lit the grain mouthway
straightaway a sand or strangled mind is made
the stinging springs of valleys opened eternal
never given in dry ribs
and that it originates again
and that it takes the cord and leaves it hammered and
    defenceless
you win above those craggy eyes
the structure that of falcon that of silver

ovunque vada la cenere d'ambiente contro
i sassolini tacciono atteriti che in non posso sparire
nemmeno quell'agganciare l'occhio
la mano che agita
sul vento piomba in corrente e si tocca
ho un altro ovale che dire orizzonte
quando è secco davanti alla bocca
stessa sete dei corridori che staccano

wherever goes the ash of the atmosphere against
the small stones become silent terrified wherein I
    cannot disappear
not even that hooking of the eye
the hand that waves
on the wind sinks into the current and touches itself
I have another oval which says horizon
when it's dry at the front of the mouth
same thirst of runners who drop out

ogni cosa si attesta nel fumo e poi non rilancia
quante volte c'era un pesce a strabiliare le rughe
nel cerchio ogni volta segreto
appaiono i cerchi di grande forza minore
per tutto lo stucco la corsa
sprigiona il nebuloso invito alle catene
e la sorella ripassa e nell'insieme
un genio di foglie da masticare

each thing lines up in the smoke and then can't restart
how many times there was a fish to astonish the folds
in the circle each time secret
with less grand power the circles appear
the rush for the entire sculpture
frees the cloudy invitation to chains
and my sister comes by again and all whole
an inheritance of leaves to chew upon

scosso il calendario della trama
il cartoccio lievita poi s'inabissa
altri uccelli li ossido
per chiamarla cera se l'arrembaggio dei piedi si assesta
neve foglie numero di foglie sempre grande
cosa trascino nella tasca che tu possa guardare i fiori
e soffiare la statua sotto la ciglia ferma

having shaken the calendar of the plot
the wrapping rises then sinks
other birds I tarnish
to call it wax if the scrambling of feet settles
snow leaves the number of leaves always great
thing I drag in my pocket so you can look at the
    flowers
and whisper the statue under still eyelashes

non puoi essere il primo liquido e basta
salivo
non per controllare le rondini
ma per sentire un trillo
trapassarmi
da una vasca immobile nella sera del passato
tutto è qui in un pugno di donne
con gli uomini
tutti posti quadrati in là
e quadrato in sé
fumo dispari incorniciati

you can't be the first liquid and enough
I was climbing
not to monitor the swallows
but to hear a trilling
pass through me
from a motionless stroll in the evening of the past
everything here in a fist of women
with the men
all placed and squared over there
and fixed in themselves
framed uneven smoke

e ultimi sono occhi

e tutti i colori sono sandali
all'arrivo
stella vuota come tutto bianco ancora
mentre io scelgo pietra tra
due piume una si staccherà

and last come the eyes

and all the colours are light shoes
on arrival
the empty star as if still all white
while I choose stone between
two feathers one will fall away

dico e mescoliamo le mani
prendo da una nuvola
ma poi la cenere riempie
marta sassi
ecco chi ho amato su una riga
muovere un fulmine
che una bambola che rimbalzi sulle colonne
si sporge la poesia e lo dico io
se polvere e pari si ammantano
frenando con la mia carta
al cielo dirò se poi…ho l'occhio gonfio
i vecchi scartano e fischiano al miele
l'aqua che asciuga ridendo

I say and we mix our hands
I take from a cloud
but then the ash fills
war's tombstones
here is the one I loved on a line
move a streak of lightning
so that a doll you bounce off the columns
poetry leans out I tell you
if dust and the like are in a mantle
my paper as a brake
I will tell the sky then... I have a swollen eye
the old people unwrap and whistle at the honey
the water which dries laughing

alti coperchi come una primavera chiusa in sfera di fumo
sarebbero calessi il pensiero pugno nelle maschere bagnate
..........in una....
...i tagli dei posti....
...disegno grigio: il legno: la fuga più importante
i poeti è come dico io
avanza di sbieco la farina poi è bambina a toccarti i capelli
finchè la cadenza ragguinge il buio
i ragni sono lanciati per la mamma   è   domenica

high covers as if closing spring in a sphere of smoke
would-be cabriolets the thought punched through the wet
    masks
......in a....
...the cuts of places....
...grey design: wood: the most essential escape
poets it is as I say
some flour's left askew then it's a small girl who touches
    your hair
until its falling reaches into the dark
the spiders are hurled for mother it's Sunday

le battute che appaiono nel seme
che tagliò i canali in carta e vestiti
noi ameremo più volte
di più è una roccia a mollare
la torcia sul viso degli interi sapori
o colombe! gelidamente!
tutto ciò con cui non so più stare
e simili vapori ne chiamano il coriandolo
eccoti il bacio che saltella più volte

che avanza senza dire niente
l'elastico del trono

the jokes which appear in the seed
which cut canals in paper and clothes
we will love more times
more is a rock to soften
the torch on the face of entire tastes
o doves! icily!
everything I no longer know how to remain with
and similar vapours are called coriander
here is the kiss for you which leaps several times

which advances without saying anything
the elastic of the throne

ai suoi denti leggeri nel seguire la foresta
chi l'ha pensato nelle scorze ha visto
come quando affisso sul mucchio
e te ne vai dal lato del timbro senza terra
allora si attacca alle lastre la testa
sfondata dalle corse paglierine
ma non vuoi sibilare per conto tuo

metallo che vai a sud!

ciliegio che stai a nord!

io ti do una bufera e bianco

in following the forest to his light teeth
who has thought in the bark has seen
as when I stick myself to the pile
and you go off to one side of the stamp without earth
so then it attaches itself to the slab the head
smashed in by straw-coloured races
but you don't want to whistle on your own account

metal which goes to the south!

cherry which stays in the north!

I will give you a snowstorm and white

un lato bianco con tronchi
guizzano insieme
e pigiama e carote urtano le pietre
io stesso entrato nella violenza circolare
poeta! adesso attingo da un uomo che cammina lentamente
e respingo il risparmio che si produce sull'aspro della
    fionda
ma chi sa tornare
che cade indifferentemente tra i pezzi del diluvio
e per sempre ama la morte di neve

one white side with logs
dart past together
and pyjamas and carrots crash against stone
I too have entered this circular violence
poet! now I have attained the stage of the man who
    walks slowly
and I push away the saving produced in the bitterness
    of a sling
but who knows how to return
that falls indifferently between the pieces of the flood
and loves forever the death of snow

e via verso un'arrampicata nell'aria
lasciata cadere la mano nel diluvio
le foglie sono dunque intitolate
navi degli attrezzi e lampade amare come sono
io so descriverti infinitamente in giardino
col ladro della pace che girava nel lato interessato
su questo tavolo ronza la ghiaia
le trombe dei posti micidiali

and away towards a climbing into the air
having let your hand slip into the flood
leaves therefore bear a title
boats of tools and lamps to love as they are
I know how to describe you infinitely in the garden
with the thief of peace who hangs around the
    profitable side
on this table the buzz of pebbles
the trumpets of murderous places

deviando per le stanze erano uomini e vapori
un cerchio falso
eppure mi domando una mosca per salire
rotta e ruggine
come le foglie che in lui
possono sbarrarsi e dare pane alle costole
cos'era quel seme
piange silenziosamente e io m'incateno al fuoco
e quando sarà
un giglio sulle spalle mi fa male il viso

they were men and vapours on a detour through the
    rooms
a false circle
nevertheless I ask for a fly to climb
the rot and rust
as the leaves which in him
can lock themselves in and give bread to his ribs
what was that seed
weeps in silence and I chain myself to fire
and when will it be
a lily on my shoulder, my face with its sudden pain

FROM *Fire Births*

stella polare

a mia sorella Adriana

l'infanzia le farfalle mi uccisero gli occhi
forse come le pezze che piangono nel mezzo
perdendo l'accogliente ciclone
perché anche la poltiglia è semplice

la donna perfettamente tesa come per polvere
di un ragno spaventato dalla bocca
la fronte si è abbassata
fino all'assalto delle tenaglie
sono venuto qua
dico vado e vado a colpire quei pali
e nulla il tempo

polar star

for my sister Adriana

childhood the butterflies killed my eyes
perhaps like the patches which cry in the middle
and lose the welcoming cyclone
because even the pulp is simple

the woman perfectly stretched as if for dust
of a spider frightened by the mouth
the forehead is lowered
until the pincers' assault
I came here
I say I go and I go to strike those poles
and nothing the time

c'è una bocca che apre passando
tu che li hai visti
arrestano un attimo la danza
li ha colpiti gelando
donne che la pietra dal fumo
erano incantate

there's a mouth which passing opens
you who have seen them
they stop the dance for a moment
it's struck them freezing
women that stone from the smoke
has enchanted

carnevale

all'orizzonte nemmeno
ero muto ma tenevi le perle
e si raccolgono intorno con un tuono
l'aquila piccola trasporterà gli stracci
mare
non ho sommato le onde
solo fuoco con gli occhi le lapidi
passando fra gli uomini
le lacrime con un gran saliscendi

carnival

on the horizon not even
was I mute but you held the pearls
and they gather around a thunderclap
the small eagle will carry the rags
sea
I haven't added up the waves
only fire with eyes the headstones
passing among men
the tears with a great rise and fall

io non sento che macinate
aria e fragole
dentro il mio occhio
la confusione dei solchi
zeppi di ferro
al cono che li appende
nemmeno noi calpestavamo
il sorriso
che al pendolo
ritiravo nella mia pancia
una terra di morti
attentamente comincia ed è fuoco
più di – ebbe le mani staccate dal corpo –
non so le nuvole

I feel nothing but minced
air and strawberries
inside my eye
the confusion of furrows
packed with iron
up to the cone which hangs them
even we didn't trample on
the smile
which at the swing of the pendulum
I pulled back into my belly
a land of dead
carefully begins and it's fire
more than – the hands having been torn from the body –
I don't know the clouds

il grande libro

molti sono di neve ma prudenti
tutto ciò che è stroncato è perfetto
parole si è detto dicono
formandosi nell'acqua dentro di loro
si posano sul marmo
è la nuvola il reato il muro dei cinque capelli
non si è con la luce la bolla fa
non puoi più riassumere l'inverno tomba

the great book

many are made of snow but prudent
all that is broken is perfect
words one says they say
forming in the water inside them
they lay themselves on marble
it's the cloud the crime the wall of five hairs
we are not with the light the bubble makes
you can no longer resume the gravestone winter

il cammino

arrivata fin qui
era la mosca che dorme con sé
tu del tuo volto facevi un pilastro
muovendo le mani
il fiore che risale la pace
l'eredità della notizia è forte
è immenso il fermarsi a dipingere
le cose che non verranno possono dirlo

the walk

having arrived here
it was the fly which slept with itself
you with your face made a pillar
moving your hands
the flower which climbs peace
the legacy of news is strong
it's immense the stopping to paint
the things which won't come can tell us

con l'amore

quando la neve giunge
come le palafitte degli occhi del nero degli occhi
le parole qualcosa volevano dire
la prima cosa intera
e la cenere in mille modi
raggiunge la tartaruga
la lascia coi fiori
nel tempo
nessuno nemmeno nulla ha visto

with love

when the snow reaches
like pile-dwellings of eyes of the black of eyes
words something they wanted to say
the first whole thing
and ash in a thousand ways
reaches the tortoise
leaves it with flowers
in time
no one has seen anything

il disco

quelli che sono morti
qualità che non sanno se uno è mite
gli stessi punti in corazza
la nebbia è il tuo omaggio deserto
una crepa
dove stanno per giungere a irrigare
o più o meno a sferzare
le parole che hanno attratto
la processione di sacchi
se uno non ha come timbra il medesimo luoghi
le piccole dosi di sputo
sul cavallo
ossia vissuto qui
in fondo
quanto va avanti

the disk

those who are dead
quality they don't know if one is meek
the same points in armour
the mist is your deserted homage
a crack
where they're about to arrive to irrigate
or more or less to lash
the words which have attracted
the procession of sacks
if one doesn't frank oneself places
the small doses of spit
on the horse
or else having lived here
deep down
how far it goes ahead

frammento grande

è cielo molto tempo fa ne aveva avuto
chi può dare alla schiena
ora se guardo il fiume che il sonno
ha detto non saper bastonare
di una lacrima improvvisa

great fragment

it's sky long ago it had some
who can turn their back
now if I look at the river which sleep
has told me not knowing how to strike
of an unexpected tear

signori di notte sicura

l'airone grande
più piano e ancora più piano
può darsi me e la sola acqua si orienta
signori date la gioia senza manifestare mosche
le nuvole che sono di grandezza parola assente
lasciate questo insieme
la ressa di un bastoncino
non voglio voltarmi se è la luce secca

gentlemen of the safe night

the great heron
softly and still more softly
perhaps me and the water only finds its bearings
gentlemen give joy without showing flies
the clouds which have greatness absent word
leave it together
the crowd on a little stick
I don't want to turn around if the light is dry

la barricata dei punti

il chiodo svanito in noi
e nell'acqua
come ad avere il sole
i capelli con topolini gialli
resurrezioni per niente di fatto in fila
e tegole di cioccolato
il compito dei colori
rompiamo i più pallidi
che voltano le pietre
viste le ombre
può darsi del cuore

the spiked barricade

the nail vanished inside us
and in the water
like having the sun
the hair with little yellow mice
resurrections came to nothing real in a row
and tiles of chocolate
the task of colours
let's smash the most pallid
which the stones turn
having seen the shadows
of the heart perhaps

nati incendio

*a Marta Bertamin*i

quando tutto s'impiglia
ma non visi buoni
freddo come poteva essere
hai parlato
con tanto legno alle tue spalle più distante
io sono immobile
si alza il pomeriggio e il verme di miele viene via
ecco una luna una valigia
com'è tua madre
come la diagonale
tutto se non fosse stretto
sarebbe di ruotare in dono alla minuscola valle
ma sono sordo ai capelli della regina
la ruggine è bella
cosí ti lascio
piazza
nel fuoco che balbetta
infine
perché è anch'esso il fiume più leale
tolta dai guanti
senti non senti l'urto

fire births
for Marta Bertamini

when everything is entangled
but not some good faces
cold as it could get
you spoke
with much wood at your shoulders more distant
and me motionless
the afternoon rises and the worm of honey comes away
here is a moon a suitcase
as your mother
is like the diagonal
everything if it wasn't so tight
would be to rotate as a gift into the miniscule valley
but I'm deaf to the hairs of the queen
rust is beautiful
so I'm leaving you
piazza
in the stuttering fire
finally
because it too is the most loyal river
removed from the gloves
you feel you don't feel the blow

la paglia che scompone

il lume è interno
ha le spugne ai lati
e beve l'acqua fucilata da piccoli roditori
forse vaga così sulle parole
una goccia distingueva il sogno
poi niente
stai attenta alla morte
nei bicchieri tutto il suo galoppo è grigio
il mare lascia una copia
delle stelle sul torace
se ti ho mai vista davanti
piove con i tagli per gli occhi

the straw which comes apart

the light is internal
it has sponges at its sides
and drinks water shot by small rodents
perhaps vague this way over the words
a drop distinguished the dream
then nothing
watch out for death
in glasses its whole gallop is grey
the sea leaves a copy
of stars on the chest
if I have ever seen you in front of me
it rains with cuts for eyes

soffocanti

cosa cerchi
parli di una tomba
il titolo della festa del mondo
pietre in sospensione acuta
rispondeva una donna da distanze solubili
quando più che altro
il falco viene a cuocere i piedi
sono le pistole di gelo che irrompono
l'ombra a tagliarmi

suffocating

what are you looking for
you speak of a tomb
the title of the world festival
stones in acute suspension
responded a woman from soluble distances
when more than anything
the hawk comes to cook the feet
these are the pistols of ice which explode
the shadow to cut me

il castello della fine

le macchie hanno più breve
mai da un passero
con lo stesso calcio che può dare il mondo
l'incamminarmi è deciso in un pulviscolo atroce
e mi fermo da te
non ho imitato la morte era solo una vela che tenevo ferma
per questo stringe la spina
e nera è più bella che altrove
ma ora ripestando
sete che vedono tutti e due e intanto te
quando sapremo mancare
un sasso ci lascerà improvvisamente
è infilato nella schiena
ciechi che nascono sotto l'asfalto
magra prima scienza

the castle at the end

the stains have briefer
never from a sparrow
with the same kick that the world can give
my setting off to walk is decisive in a terrible dust
and I stop beside you
I haven't imitated death it was only a sail which I held
    still
for this it squeezes the thorn
and black is more beautiful than elsewhere
but now treading once more
thirst which we both see and you meanwhile
when we know how to die
a stone will leave us suddenly
piercing the spine
blind who are born under asphalt
first thin science

nella cosa
per te che hai appena le mani sul tavolo
il mondo deserto discende dal cielo
con metà acqua e occhio di benzina
non volevo sapere
volevo morire fra le due lastre
perché avere il collo veloce
e come pinocchio affossava i dipinti
se luce e tempo sono le mie palline intorno
giovane zingaro hai fatto nascere
qui io ti libero
e piangi questo resto
perché con unico che mi abbassi le labbra

in the thing
for you who have your hands only just on the table
the deserted world descends from the sky
with half-water and eye of petrol
I didn't want to know
I wanted to die between the two panes
because having a fast neck
and as pinocchio pushed down the paintings
if light and season are my marbles around
young traveller you've helped it come to life
here I let you go free
and you cry these remains
because with one alone you lower my lips

finite e vedete quello che non c'è più davvero
bufalo del tempo bianco furioso
so che saranno morte le onde
e io ne ricavo
il silenzio che indirizza le punte
e non è vero neanche il silenzio
ero un bambino
all'acqua infilata nel fumo
la luce è nel peso
infinito perfetto chiunque
palco lo stesso quale divento sereno

finish and see what's no longer really there
buffalo of white furious season
I know the waves will be dead
and I take from them
the silence which addresses the tips
and even the silence isn't true
I was a child
in the water that was inside the smoke
the light is in the weight
perfect infinite whoever
the same stage where I become serene

la statua

è come neve
le foglie
come zen sul tappeto
le dita suonarono a spiga
le spinte in ogni acqua dai dolci improvvisi
che le parole rasentano
sono false false
è vera
come lauretta prima delle scure
non attraverso il tempo nessuna lacrima
solo appoggia il disco suona
io esplodo e gli stracci intorno mi respingono
allontano le nuvolette
padri e madri in mongolfiera
sono guarito

the statue

it's like snow
the leaves
like zen on the rug
the fingers sounded wheat ears
the thrusts in each water from sudden sweetnesses
which words brush
they're false false
it's true
as little laura before the axe falls
throughout time no tears
just put on the record and play
I burst and the rags around push me away
I banish the little clouds
fathers and mothers in an air balloon
I'm healed

da strettissima a luminosa
non vuol essere sangue nè cartolina
tacche
per te che sarai presto paradiso e acqua
come donna che toglie la cenere alle unghie
e bambina mi parla
un momento cosí sarà
paura che suonino alla porta

from most narrow to the luminous
not wanting to be blood or picture card
notches
for you who will soon be paradise and water
like a woman who removes the ash from her nails
and a little girl speaks to me
a moment like that will be
fear that they will ring at the door

vetrine

decidono per il veleno
ancora meglio che distribuire
e tu con le mani dei rami soffocati
se ammirasse il deserto
la spada
stessa ciliegia gli dice
mangio come i serpenti falciati dal fuoco

shop windows

they decide on poison
better still than distribution
and you with hands of suffocated branches
if it admired the desert
the sword
same cherry tells him
I eat like serpents ripped by fire

i chiodi con gli occhi che vedevi
e tutto quanto in semplice ordine
all'inizio della gola
faremo domani un fiocco
vede baciare le cassette d'aria
in questo tempo ho mosso
non di più
non è troppo per dire esplosioni
in fila dalle foglie
riceve il battesimo
madre raddoppiata
pavone di polvere

the nails with your eyes that you saw
and everything in a clear order
at the beginning of the throat
tomorrow we'll make a rosette
sees kissing the little boxes of air
I've moved in this time
no more
it isn't too much to say explosions
in a line of leaves
receives the baptism
doubled mother
peacock of dust

il primo dolore non previsto è bellezza
io di fronte a te
sono giù dalla roccia con l'occhio dei pupazzi
posso lanciarmi
i reflessi del sole
uno per uno vivi
mentre parli col tuo volto a scodellare
donna dal convertire in neve il tuo sorso
cammina poi guarda
se c'è un'asticciola per morire
il pensiero dita
è qua io sono tinto e tutto
e là mangiando aria con un breve distacco
un tuono nella stanza bianca
le storie di ieri

the first unexpected pain is beauty
me facing you
I'm down from the rock with the eye of a puppet
I can throw myself
the sun's reflections
one by one alive
while you speak with your face to dish up
woman with your sip to convert into snow
walk then see
if there's a stick to die with
the thought finger
and here I am dyed and all
and there eating air with a brief detachment
a thunderclap in the white room
the stories of yesterday

intanto oggi che si accucciano i levrieri
intorno alle fontane il rumore è più forte
le cose sommerse con una carezza vedono il lago
e tutto può bastare per le svolte
per quei puntini
forse la bambina che guarda la sua ombra
è contenta del pane
io sto qui nel calco e resto a smistare

in the meantime today since the greyhounds crouch
around the fountains the noise is greater
things submerged with a caress they see the lake
and everything can be enough for the turnings
for those tiny points
perhaps the girl who looks at her shadow
is happy with the bread
I'm here in the imprint and remaining to unravel

avanzo con un boato interno
visto mormorare e stamparsi
la talpa scesa dal cielo
le troppe dita dell'autobus
ancora uno spazio
tuttavia buio e per i biscotti condurre le barche
la testa al cuscino
fuggono le scarpe orientali
tu diverso dai colori
e sempre nel ruscello dove volto i capelli
perché un cerchio sia più amico
alle dita e precedente al respiro
i funghi in armonia coi tetti
per quanta notte io sia caduto la rampa
non ignorare questo

I advance with an inner rumble
seen murmuring and printing itself
the mole come down from the sky
the too many fingers of the bus
still a space
yet dark and with biscuits leading the boats
the head to the cushion
oriental shoes escape
you different from the colours
and always in the stream where I turn your hair
so that a circle is more friend
to the fingers and comes before breath
the mushrooms in harmony with roofs
however much night I have fallen the steps
don't turn away from this

quando il mondo si spacca
io pennello in voi la foca del mio cuore storto
un rettilineo lunghissimo
la barca che polverizza gli occhi
ma ora è dev'essere inteso il pane
costando neve e bricioli castani in fiore
ombra che decide ombra
era una notte
attualmente inteso marmo
più di tanto in su degli stracci sapiente

when the world cracks open
I paint in you the seal of my crooked heart
such a long straight
the boat which pulverizes our eyes
but now it is must be understood the bread
costing snow and brown crumbs in flower
shadow deciding shadow
it was one night
now agreed marble
more than far above a few rags knowing

attendendo il sonno alla radice dei capelli
non si può
né marcire lo stupore nel guanto assolato
ma ci saranno altre code
altri elastici induriti
e ci sia
tuono impazzito che vuoi del poeta senza mano

waiting for sleep at the hair root
one cannot
nor rot the astonishment in the sunny glove
but there will be other codes
other hardened elastics
and that there be
crazed thunder what do you want of the poet without
   hands

THE AUTHOR

Ivano Fermini (1948-2004) was born in San Paolo, a small village near Bolzano in the Alpines. Most of his adult life he lived with his sister in a flat in a working-class area of San Siro in Milan. He suffered from recurring bouts of mental illness. Towards the end of the 1970s he joined the 'Niebo' group, which centred around the poet Milo De Angelis, and included Emi Rabuffetti, Antonio Mungai, Alberto Schieppati, Giancarlo Pontiggia, Cesare Lievi, Marta Bertamini and Roberto Mussapi. The *Niebo* magazine, founded by De Angelis, ran to nine issues from 1977 to 1980, and published work inspired by visionary poets, such as William Blake, Gérard de Neval, and Arthur Rimbaud. Fermini himself was especially drawn to the work of Paul Celan. He would go on to publish two collections, *Bianco allontanato* (*Banished White*) in 1985, and in 1990, *Nati incendio* (*Fire Births*). Both these collections are now long out of print. He remains relatively unknown, both inside and outside Italy. It is hoped that this collection will bring his work to both an Italian- and English-speaking audience.

The Translator

Ian Seed teaches Creative Writing at the University of Chester, and has also lectured in Italian Language and Literature at the University of Lancaster. He is a poet, critic, fiction writer, editor and translator. His latest collection of poetry is *The Underground Cabaret* (Shearsman, 2020). He is a contributing editor of *The Fortnightly Review*.

THE CATALOGUE OF ODD VOLUMES

Through 1 September 2022

1. **Screeds** of Stephen Wiest. (July 2013) Price: $10.95 | £7.90

2. **Dostoyevski and the Religion of Suffering** by E-M de Vogüé. (November 2013) Price: $9.95 | £6.95

3. **The Invention of the Modern World by** Alan Macfarlane. (April 2014) Price: $16.95 | £9.45

4. **Labyrinths & Clues** by Alan Wall. (May 2014) Price: $22.00 | £10.75

5. **Helen** by Oswald Sickert, introduction by Denis Boyles. (September 2014) Price: $12.95 | £8.00

6. **Telegrams from the City under Siege** by Marco Genovesi, in English and Italian; translated by Hoyt Rogers. (August 2015) Price: $15.00 | £9.95

7. **The Fortnightly Reviews: Poetry Notes 2012-2014** by Peter Riley (October 2015) Price: $17.50 | £12.95

8. **Science and Religion** by Ferdinand Brunetière; translated by Erik Butler (April 2016) Price: $15.00 | £10.00.

9. **Rejected! Literary Failure and My Contribution to It** by Stephen Wade (July 2017) Price: $19.95 | £15.00

10. **Verisimilitudes** by James Gallant. (May 2018) Price: $15.00 £10.00

11. **Truinas: 21 April 2001,** by Philippe Jaccottet, translated by John Taylor. June 2018. Price (hardcover edition only): $25.00 £18.00

12. **Walter Benjamin: An Arcade of Reflections** by Alan Wall. June 2018. Price: $12.95 £ 9.50

13. **Consciousness (with Mutilation)** by Anthony Howell. (180 pp, paper, January 2019.) $18.00 £15.00.

14. **A Notebook of Clouds** by Pierre Chappuis, translated from the French by John Taylor. With **A Notebook of Ridges** by John Taylor. (160 pp, paper, May 2019.) $16.95 £12.95 €15.77.

15. **Credo: Exhibits and Other Poems,** by Stephen Wiest (105 pp, paper, June 2020). $16.95 £13.38 €15.84

16. **Why Are You Here? Very Brief Fictions**, by Simon Collings (104 pp, paper, November 2020). $16.95 £12.95 €15.77

17. **Midnight of the Sublime: Essays and Reviews**, by Alan Wall (290 pp, paper, March 2021) $23.95 £18.00 €20,90

18. **Pedraterra & Angleterre: Two Fables**, by Anthony Rudolf (190pp, paper, June 2021) $17.95 £14.95

19. **Four Times EightyOne: bespoke stories**, by Michelene Wandor (200 pp, paper, October 2021) $17.95, £15.95

20. **Buster Brown's America: Recollections, Reveries, Reflections** — and incorporating *This Old Writer: A Journal of a Plague Year*, by Igor Webb (298 pp, paper, April 2022) $17.95 £15.95

21. **Varieties of Homage** by John Matthias (179 pp, paper, June 2022) $17.95 £15.95

22. **The River Which Sleep Has Told Me** by Ivano Fermini, translated from Italian by Ian Seed. (120 pp, paper, October 2022.) $17.95 £16.95

Order online: http://fortnightlyreview.co.uk/odd-volumes/ or through your local bookseller.

Odd Volumes are published for subscribers to *The Fortnightly Review*.
For details, write info@fortnightlyreview.co.uk